Aha! and Ha-Ha

(Melpomene and Thalia)

By Lisbeth L. McCarty

Table of Contents

Aha and Ha-Ha: Why The Title?

By Lisbeth L. McCarty

Some readers believe that poetry should always cause deep searching of the soul, making them feel emotions, maybe melancholy or deep thought, or make them exclaim, "Aha!" Some readers appreciate poetry that causes glee to the soul, maybe filling them with happiness or merely a smile, or make them exclaim, "Ha-Ha!."

Some readers appreciate both styles. There is room in this world for both "Aha" and "Ha-Ha!" poetry, as well as every other kind of poetry in existence.

The two masks of comedy and tragedy are named for the Greek Muses named Melpomene and Thalia. Melpomene has the sad face, and Thalia has the smile.

We may love poems as serious
As Poe's raven tapping
We may love silly poems
Lear's work can make us happy

Frost fills us with wonder
As he takes us through the snow
Nash can make us laugh
With his "quicker liquor" joke

While Angelou discovered
Why the caged bird sings
A boy named Sue amused us
In the words of Silverstein

Hughes made his analogy
About a raisin in the sun
Riley said the children
"Has the mostest fun!"

Dickinson is serious,
Hope perching in her soul
Carroll's oysters took a walk
For about a mile or so

Sometimes, we pretend to soar
To the heights of well-known poets
Sometimes, we see the world
And all that life can show us

The ego is no problem
When dreaming sets us free
At times, pretending is better
Than life in reality

In The Shadows

Tonight in the shadows, I saw a white ghost
And a girl was swallowing tears when she spoke
And a voice was chanting -- it rang in my head
But the face of reason was asleep with the dead

If I could just see you one more time again
Maybe you'd love me, or at least be my friend
But the whispers I heard that I thought might be you
Were trees with the sound of the wind rustling through

The white ghost was a guard, just passing by
And the girl with the tears was myself as I cried
And the voice was conviction, judging my case
But the face of reason would not awake

Later in life, Mom never left the house
Except to go to her grandson's Little League games
He was the golden child among grandchildren
She'd climb through mountains to see him at bat
Sometimes, I went, too
Sure, I like baseball
But I mainly went
To spend time with Mother
I sat in the stands, sweat pouring from my brow
July is no time for the weak at a ball park
I drank lots of water
To try to defray a heat stroke
Mom had her own method of coping
She wore capri pants
She laughed at the fashion world's suggestion
That a woman past the age of 73 should not wear capri pants
She did not care that the part of her legs that showed
Were vein-filled indications of her hard-scrabble life
But for me, the theoretical leg maps
Reminded me of Mom's vulnerability
Reminded me that Mom won't be here forever
Reminded me that Mom is a mere mortal
Reminded me that Mom has faded beauty
And reminded me that tears are salty

Past the crystal glean of the snow banks
You catch my eye, bombshell not of a woman,
But of a man wrapped in a winter parka,
Sparkling blue eyes peek out from the handsome face
Framed by thick fur to shut out the blizzard
You laugh and say the fur is not real,
So I know I could love you
Yet, you are as troubling as black ice,
Not someone to keep close,
That rare species of a prism growing dim, then dying
No longer reflecting light, a bleak moon with no man in it,
Forever leading a double life
A time bomb for rejecting those needing love
Let's meet on neutral ground
For less than either of us see as a bargain
You are getting away with bringing in the firewood
As a synonym for love, yet it is really
Just frostbite you are fending off
Smarter than most psychopaths living in an alien land
Always speaking another language that cannot be understood
Other than to be a constant wind chill of unsubtle harassment
We sip champagne from Mason jars
Severing the spine of chicness
Two torsos of psychopaths living together
Nice to see you again as we play this game of cat and mouse
Sentenced to a non-parole period of living in a new home
Always hopeful and yet, not so
You almost got away with the pretensions
Of the emotions of a good man
What lurks? The devil's work is full of twisted desires.
Two is too many generations under one roof, so I leave
The freeze of snowflakes
Pierce through my silly-looking balaclava
I turn back to look, but the curtains are drawn
There is no "our" any more
As I walk away, my boots make deep patterns in the snow

Urban Life

Skyline full of buildings
Where is the real sky?

Marquees of celebrities
Where are the real stars?

A city pulses with feeling
Where is the real emotion?

Racers without faces
Where are the real people?

There is odd comfort
In the obscurity.

My Personal Reminder

Even today, the words ring true
Pride comes before a fall
I didn't fall; you shoved me down,
Tried to shatter me into a million fears
I was selected for apparent vulnerability
Just flesh and bones to you, ashes to ashes, dust to dust
You targeted a perceived weakness of your prey,
But I worked so intensely on the
Puzzle of missing pieces,
The psychopathy of your soul,
The existential potential
Never dismissed with a kiss of betrayal
Selfishness drives helplessness
You do not get to decide
Whether I exist
I got up
Coward that you are
You fled into the dark night
Leaving your knife behind
As my personal reminder
Of survival

How did you sense
Through my brave front
That a soul existed
Underneath it all?

How did you hear
Through all the white noise
My still-beating heart
Underneath it all?

How did you see
Through all the disguises
The fear in my eyes
Underneath it all?

How did you taste
Through all the lipstick
My quest for love
Underneath it all?

How did you smell
Through the mist of doubt
The answers I needed
Underneath it all?

You touched me
Underneath it all
You touched me
And that was enough

When a Peach is Like a Human

The ripe peach is ombre, both inside and out,
Luscious orange hues fade into muted reds on the outside
Inside, the radiance of the maroon pit fades into light red,
Then returns to the
Orange of its coat
Yet, sometimes, the peach begins to rot from the inside,
Hiding its negative under a coat of colors
Occasionally, peaches are like human beings
Sometimes, the ones so beautiful to behold on the outside
Are rotting on the inside
Let us judge only
By the true character inside
And not be led astray by an amazing exterior
Beware, but love your fellow man
Including the bad peaches
But keep your distance for your own sanity
And, yet, still love

Movement as Art

The amber tones of the harp-like lyre
Move my soul into love territory
I am compelled to jump to my feet,
Spin in pirouettes, leap through the air in tour jetés,
Pas de bourrée couruas in pointe shoes
As the notes intensify
In line with the choreography.
I love my involvment
In the stunning aert form
That inspires all parts of the body to move
To all worlds of music
Terpsichore is my Muse,
Dance is my primary reason for being,
My everything
After the music ends,
I take a bow
And luxuriate in the intoxicating aroma
Of the red, pink, yellow, and white roses
Thrown onto the wooden stage
I will return the next day
To repeat my ballerina actions
And visit pure happiness, again

Throbbing Heart

He asked me to be his editor
His writing is full of stilted jumbled stupid
Crazy ramblings without proper punctuation
Yet somehow portraying the throbbing heart of life
The anguish is there
Fat, greedy fingers of emotions leap from the page
Clasping around my brain
Strangling me with the absolute chaos
Of marred perfection
No editing needed

Solstice

Leaves float on the surface of the backyard runoff
As reminders that flash storms followed by rainbows
Are omens,
Warnings to be wary of mystical promises about the future.
A black cat curls on the deck,
Resembling a hibernating bear cub.
Smells of a neighbor's charcoaled dinner offerings
Waft on the back of a warm, summer breeze,
Along with the clinking of glasses
And voices talking and laughing,
Proof eternal of a nearby patio party
To which I was not invited.
The revelers and I are separated by privacy fences
And seasons and numbers.
They are many in June, but I am one, alone, in December.
I stand frozen in a winter twilight that is punctuated by falling
snowflakes,
Reminding me that my life is regulated
Like the required syllables of a haiku.
My weariness drives me back inside
To the solitude of a cold house.

Tennis Love

When he says, "Te Amo,"
He means, "No Te Amo."
This is something I know
Because his pawing and clawing
Will never imbed in a relationship.
In his head,
He is a confirmed bachelor
And I am a passenger
On a train to nowhere
Intimate acts for him
Are like playing tennis
He only needs a partner for a game
He and the partner do not even have to like each other;
He just wants to play
Intimate acts for me
Are like invitations to commitment
I would be planning the wedding invitations in my head
Who wants to be on the wrong end
Of a score of 30-love?
I try to run, but I am frozen

Progressive abolitionist parents
Encouraged Mary Walker's education,
Propelling her to study long hours
To become a medical doctor
She found dresses too restrictive to movement,
Solving the problem by wearing a "Bloomer costume"
Nothing more than pants underneath her dress
Which caused the disdain of the haughty and ignorant people
Mary was not persuaded to give up her chosen uniform
She was scrappy
The Civil War was a world in chaos
Mary's desire to join the fight as a military surgeon
To heal the wounded
Was extinguished by existing conventions
Which would not allow
A woman to serve in such a government position
Instead, Mary, heart of a patriot, served as a civilian
Treating the wounded on the battlefield
sewing flesh wounds back together
With rudimentary instruments
And scrappiness
Captured by the South and made a prisoner of war,
She survived four months on hard tack and hope
In 1865, she was then the only woman to be bestowed
The Medal of Honor
In 1917, that honor was rescinded under the realization
That Dr. Walker had never been military personnel,
Despite her best efforts to do so
Continuing to flout convention,
Mary outright refused to return the medal
No illusions and delusions would manipulate her mind
She was still scrappy
Mary proudly wore the un-returned medal until she died
a mere two years later.
In 1977, the honor of Dr. Walker's name was restored
An ending she could only know
From her grave

The Necessity of Rain

After every rainfall,
I go outside to absorb
The air's invisible ions of refreshment,
Soft-Breeze appetizers for happiness

The gentle, liquid sunshine
Is the entrée of magical solutions
My sight absorbs water beads on leaves,
A factor of deliciousness

Hearing a whippoorwill,
I yoga-breath my quest for hope
The bird's call is relentless,
"This is fine. This is fine."

The liquid sunshine dessert
Of all the misty aftermath
Satisfies my confined brain
And banishes my loneliness

The weatherman predicts
Drizzling showers on Tuesday
I can only pray
That the rain comes

Wintergreen Kisses

Ready to merge
And make gel-red wishes
Let's try listening
In time for fire play

Long days ahead
Of rock-gray sadness
Schedule of dotted-line checks
Balances of slate wisdom

If based on another
Pink happiness fades
Our paths intertwine
In the burgundy pain

The results are pleasing
Hands in blue folds
Love without words
Wintergreen kisses

Thoughts to Banish

Sailing Key Largo
Yielded nothing more than
The nondisclosure of specific ideas about
Wanting him dead
Or suspecting that he wanted me dead
Super easy while I am partly awake, partly sleeping
To dream these thoughts
The cold, unforgiving depths of the water are
No place for a human body,
At least, hypothetically
Maybe there is no smoking gun
Maybe there never will be
But the crystal waters are hypnotizing me
With an urgency to take unfounded action
He puts his arm around me while we sit on the deck
While we watch the waves,
Everything is so peaceful,
And I know better than to tell him
My morbid thoughts
Who would ever know?

We all use words
Truths and lies
Love and much less
Purple prose for inspiration
Marginal lives for justification

We all use sight
Full and limited
Beauty and much less
Red roses for love
Eternal flames for justice

We all use hearing
Selective and demanding
The sweet tones of music
Which shatter our feelings
And belie our plans

We all use senses
Soft and hard
Exhilaration and depression
There are caring touches
Between the madness

We all use smells
Lilacs and burning tires
Enticing and revolting
Talents hidden or overflowing
With creativity or repulsion

We all use words
Yet, they are but vain

Day-Laborers and Cooks

We serve the well-suited
We cater to each need
We know their wants and desires
We know the way they bleed

Some treat us like sub-humans
Most treat us like the help
We're only there for them
They think we have no self

Let them function in the clouds
Let them continue to be blind
We know we have our thoughts
Our lives, our loves, our minds

An Obstacle to Overcome

A heartbeat of 175 beats per minute
Steers me into a fast lane of fear
Words I never wanted to hear come
From a paramedic in the ambulance
"This drug will stop your heart."
I didn't arrive on this Blue Marble to be eliminated
Was this going to be the anti-climatic death of me?
Too stunned to speak, the next words I hear
Are close to being reassuring
"Then, the drug will cause your heart to rise again
To a regular level."
Another paramedic lets me squeeze my scares and cares
Into his weathered, responsible hand
I grasp his long bony, skeletal fingers far too tightly
And hang on for dear life
Yes, dear life
That trite phrase thrown out so carelessly in my mind
Yet, what do words mean when the light dims, then goes out?
I died that night but rose from the dead
Only to discover a cardiac ablation in my future
I arose once from the dead
I shall arise again
Awaiting surgery, I see the moon from my hospital room
And it winks at me, a silent invitation to visit
And a hope for survival
And I know I will fly someday to the Sea of Tranquility
And breathe in the joy of existing

Roots
Twisted, strange, and dark,
Clutching and strangling the earth
And each other
So co-dependent

People
Enfolding themselves
Into other people,
A need for human connection
So co-dependent

Ever So Gently

When I first learned to walk,
Mama held my hand to make sure I didn't fall
When Mama forgot how to walk,
I held her hand to make sure she didn't fall

When I was a toddler,
Mama put a bib on me and wiped my mouth
As she fed me strained carrots
Now, I put a bib on Mama and wipe her mouth
When I feed her strained carrots

When I was in pre-K and put my shoes on the wrong foot
Mama corrected me on left and right, ever so gently
Now, when Mama puts her shoes on the wrong foot
I take action to right the wrong, ever so gently

When I had childhood imaginary friends
Mama indulged me
Now, when Mama has imaginary memories
I pretend they are real

When I ate lunch in elementary school
Mama put notes in the lunch box which said, "I love you."
Now, when Mama eats dinner, I say to her,
"I love you."

No notes for Mama because her eyesight has failed
And even though I speak, her ears no longer hear
Then, one day, Mama's mind left completely
Months later, the rest of her body left, too

I held her hand when it happened
In hopes she knew she was loved
Even if I couldn't keep her from falling,
I wish I could have held her hand forever

The Choreography of Chlorophyll

Leaves of cherry red, persimmon orange, and eggplant purple
Dance like puppets pulled by the invisible strings
Of the fickle wind
In a swirling choreography
Heightened by chlorophyll
Abandoning the autumn foliage
Occasionally, a leaf breaks free
To perform a complicated solo
Before being whisked back
To rejoin the circular chorus line
Do the leaves dance naively
Because they do not know
Their death looms
Or do they dance freely with full awareness
Of their inevitable fate?
Either way, the dance goes on

Cold That Warms Me

Beautiful blues of the sky
Contrast with the curved lines of
The purity of snow
Outlining the horizon
Like the softness of a kitten's coat
Iceland speaks to me
In gentle tones
Whispering, "Come, sit by the fire with me."
I obey, as if happily hypnotized,
At the wonder of the falling snow

Dolls and Daughters Are Easily Broken

She was six years old and crying
Over some real or imagined harm
For the first time in his life
He decided to try to be a father
And comfort her

He chose her favorite porcelain doll
Not by purpose but through luck
And held it out to her
To try to coax her
From her sorrow

The tears continued to fall
As she did not acknowledge his offering
How could she believe his sincerity
When he had ignored her various requests
So many times before?

When she asked him to come to her tea parties
He laughed cruelly, shooed her away
When she tried to show him her drawings
He wouldn't even turn his face
From the television

Now, he exploded in anger
That she dared to ignore his offer
Of a porcelain doll to stop her tears
He threw the doll to the ground
Shattering it into sharp pieces

The doll was fractured
Impossible to repair to full health
A symbol of the father-daughter relationship
Attempted to be built
On too little, too late

Union Between a Man and a Woman

I dream with my spirit
And forgive the snow leopards
For being my bridesmaids
Like Scarlett O'Hara
In spotted curtains
They threw away the dresses
After the ceremony

My persona is lost
In a cupcake dress
The irony of it all
Is the missing camera
Trash boxes hide
The entrance to publicity
No photos exist

In the end, I smile at the groom
And I sleep that night
As a married woman
Cocooned with my husband
Like hibernating bears
I feel comfort and love
As I watch the snow fall

Outside

Accidental Witness

They have to get those koi fish out of the pond
No one wants them killed in the fire
Can a flame burn in water?

The cause of death seemed obvious
Until the medical examiner discovered
A knife in the back of the torso

The gnome statute always seems to be laughing
As if to mock the police
For never catching the killer

Do I keep the secret
Because of the fear I feel?
Because of the cost?

I hear the sirens, watch the flames
Then, I go back to bed
And pull the cotton sheet over my head

A Cat Might Not Be a Solution

I'm being murdered
By my own introversion,
Paralyzed by an inability to communicate
With other human beings
Because someone might look at me
Someone might think I am stupid
Someone might even like me,
A horrible outcome for a hermit
I write, determined to engage
In a solitary activity, a lonely endeavor,
An immersion in an anti-social dream world,
Expressions without interaction
Maybe, I could be happy with cats
But they would ignore me
Destiny would dictate
That rejection would alienate me further
From contentment
Once, I heard a psychologist say
That introversion is fueled
By egomania,
Suffered by people who think
Too much of themselves
What do psychologists know?
Their only writing was required for a doctorate
Here kitty, kitty, kitty

The Oddity of Life

There's no rewind button in life
Chirping birds live unaware
They will chirp one last time
Ironically, birds in captivity
Have the longest life span
They do not fly free
They are not allowed to take risks
They flutter for days on end
In the confined spaces of steel cages
What kind of life is that?
Yet, in every living being
A survival instinct exists
Despite the fact that there is evil in the world
Perhaps the good outweighs the bad
Should there be begging for more time
Or just gratitude for today?

Insomnia

The breeze comes down to the valley from the mountains above
I wait all day for the gentle wind to bring the stories
That help me fall asleep long before the dawn
Sometimes, when the breeze never comes, I shut the curtain
And watch rainbow dots move through my closed eyes
For hours on end
Until the sun rises

Young Attempts

Teenager in prison
Punishment must
Fit the crime
Not lawless elsewhere

Stabbed, beaten, pushed
Nowhere to run
Nowhere to hide
Nowhere to pray

Staying alive
Such a great struggle
Escape is necessary
Mad dash for survival

Caught so quickly
Best-Laid plans
And broken hands
Doomed to fail

I miss you so much
This must be a dream
Death could not hold you
Or am I crazy?

Doves Get Better Press Than Pigeons

Awakened by the jolting ring tone
Britney singing about being toxic
The harsh perceptions clashing
With the smell of fresh clothes in the morning

Hardly time to absorb the news
Rebels fighting a wedding tradition,
Rising before dawn to release the doves
But would they fight as hard for a pigeon?

Colors on the birds may differ
But a dove is just a pigeon of a different color
I laugh at Mother Nature's joke
As I don my veil

Dreams of the Endless

Sometimes, when I sleep, I dream
About far-away places of happy absurdity,
Lands where polka-dot elephants climb Magnolia trees
The elephants lift me to them
With their pink ribbon-tied trunks,
Adorned with periwinkles
And luminescent fairies invite my elephant friends and me
To tea parties of cinnamon scones, lemon cookies,
And chocolate cakes

Then, suddenly, without warning, the nightmares come
Horrible, confusing nightmares
I awaken in fear
Sweat and tears stream down my face
My dream was of murder
And danger and entrapment and betrayal
My elephant friends are all dead,
Unmoving behemoths on the ground
The flowers are wilted, necks caved in
And the fairies have vanished, leaving behind only a tiny glow
My hand is filled with crumbs and leaves
And fairy dust and pieces of elephant tusks
I run as fast as I can
From the unnamed, unfaced evil now chasing me

Awake, I know the dream was not reality
Yet, I am still haunted by the circumstances of my slumber
I want so badly to feel safe again,
To feel loved, to feel comforted
I want my elephant, flower, and fairy friends
Around me for happiness
I do not want to fall asleep again
But Phobetor, that psychotic god of nightmares,
Is relentless in taunting me
And his brother, Morpheus, is demanding
That I return to his arms
Even though I know the deceitfulness
And catastrophe of their ways,

I succumb

Each night begins with pleasantness
But quickly becomes a ferocious cycle of nightmares,
Awakening, nightmare, awakening, nightmare
Tonight, that man in the dark ski mask outside my window
May be real after all

Fear of Truth

The demand was "Tell Me!"
But he was not pleased
When the broken silence
Was nothing more than
The creaky sound of
A little girl's voice
Speaking with such hesitation
Saying, "A ghost did it."

A vain attempt to be absorbed
Into a combo platter circle
Of permitting happiness
Allowing forgiveness
And being rewarded
For making up stuff
A place where punishment
Never exists

Hidden

The Sun Behind Me
The sun behind me
Through a swamp
Alligator smiles
Hide evil eyes

The moon before me
Through a meadow
Walking stick legs
Hide knowing minds

The ocean around me
Freedom at last
The smells of melancholy
Hide flowing tears

I learned how big the world was
When I floated one night on a moon draft
Saw the world from afar
A spinning sphere of lifetime opportunities

I discovered how vast a galaxy was
When I flew one night on a rising star
Saw the Milky Way from afar
A hazy spiral of an opaque galaxy

I found out how huge the universe was
When I held the tail of a comet
Saw all creation from afar
Breathing, loving, hurting, hoping

Yet, the moon draft chilled my legs
The rising star brought tears to my eyes
The comet tail burned my fingers
So, I shall forgot all I saw
And return to eternal loneliness

Do Not Clone Yourself

I saw a suggestion
To imagine yourself
As your own best friend
Making negative statements

The concept intends to show
The negative as silly
Leading to positivity
And banishment of the clone

The risk is doubling
All troubles and sorrows
And killing the clone
Adds to negative outlook

My Eternal Rose

I have a rose to cherish forever
Formed by sand and inclement weather
My rose has no thorns and will never die
The beauty will always satisfy

My rose, displayed nicely on a glass shelf,
Was given to me by Nature herself
Each stone petal bends in its own division
To unite together in delicate precision

Thousands of years give my rose rock its birth
I revere the stone and its infinite worth
To add to the joy of my wonderful treasure
I never had to pay for the pleasure

Here's a fact that is really quite grand
Rose rocks are found in Oklahoma sand
If you are in Oklahoma and want a rose rock
Look down at your feet, them simply take stock

Yes, you can discover your own permanent rose
Just walk by the lake and look down through your toes!

<h1 style="text-align:center">Rain, Sunshine, and Air</h1>

When the rain falls
My heart fills with joy
The world cools
And I will smile

My heart fills with joy
The sunshine follows rain
And I will smile
when I hear a robin sing

The sunshine follows rain
The air feels so positive
When I hear a bird sing
My soul fills with glee

The air feels so positive
The world is fresh
My soul fills with glee
To be part of it all

His voice has a Southern twang
That reminds me of magnolias
And white horses and cowboys
And life on the range
What would my life be
Without this ol' boy Joe?
Just knowing him
Gives a glow to my soul
Promise of adventure
His smile an escape
His eyes are pure crystals
In a delicate shape
He accepts my advances
And takes my hand
His head on my shoulder
We both understand
The cancer's advancing
We have little time left
Before he is gone
And I'm so bereft
His blonde strands of hair
have quickly vanished
He's still beautiful
Love cannot be banished
He asks me not to handle him
Like a Faberge egg
To treat him the same
But I'm a powder keg
I want a cure
I want him to heal
I want to get rid
Of the pain that I feel
The last day was happy
We laughed in the rain
He sighed and then died
And gone was his pain
My pain was eternal
My love will not die

I sit on the porch
And I cry and I cry
And I cry

The program
Deleted,
Disappeared
Thank you for watching
A life
Intended for young viewers
Cue the eerie music
Who am I?
Who are you?
Evil and good
All around
The final straw
I didn't go
I vanished

Beautiful Cold

Michigan in November
Was my first trip North
from the autumn of Oklahoma
(Which still harbored vestiges
Of the vicious summer heat)
To the bountiful snowfalls
Which bore no pretensions
About the approach of harsh winter
Frozen roads and white-outs
Greeted the senses
When the storm cleared,
The world was covered
With lush white
Houses became hills of snow
Although the cold
Chilled through the outer coverings
And straight into the soul,
The landscape was definitely
Dazzling and wonderfully cold
And I knew I'd miss the beauty of it all
When I went home

After Mother Left This Earth

I see your star too soon
Silhouetted by the moon
I see your angel wings of gold
Reflecting your kind soul

Silver highlights in your face
Shine with strength and grace
Bold stripes on your dress
Affirm your great finesse

The sky's strange orange streak
Bless the words you'll never speak
My memories shape in circles
I think of you as immortal

Your presence is so quiet
That you demand my silence
I awaken from my dream
Now, you're a distant gleam

Car on Fire

My face reddened
The car is on fire right below the pristine tennis shoe
Slung over the electrical wire
There's a code of dishonor in arson
I may be naïve, yet, I always mentally save the pictures
I dream big, I aim high
I am a fighter with a strong will to survive
I escape the flames
And watch the police artist sketch the face of my assailant
I cling to life
I know I have a brain left, but I'll avoid a mirror for now
As strong as I am, I'm also weak
Yet, I refuse to succumb
To a philosophy of, "Why me?"
The event was random, yet I live
Justice will be served because I live

Writing in a Ramshackle House

My sanity was once ironclad
But I was slowly driven mad
Searching for the perfect word
Further writing was deferred
Each fallen stone an adjective
Fleeing from the narrative
Wall-crack adverbs writhing free
Precision is my enemy
Haunted by the way I feel
Am I a ghost or am I real?

Simple Advice

The best option for each day
Is to love one another,
Going far beyond
Brother, father,
Sister, mother
Easy to preach
But hard to do
Yet, in our hearts
We know it's true

No Glory in Gangs

I'd been crying about my little brother,
Wishing he'd never joined the gang, somehow or other,
So as not to be involved in the upcoming fight,
Planned to happen just as soon as day turned into night

All day I watched Johnny, just hoping for a change
He'd been going through his weapons, acting pretty strange.
When I caught him all alone, just polishing his knife
I tried to talk to him, about how these things ain't right

About how these things hurt Ma,
About the heartbreak these wars bring
About how Ma's had enough
Since Pa disappeared some time last spring

But Johnny, he just sat there
Counting notches on his knife
And acted like this heartbreak talk
Didn't rate much in his life

I just kept on talking
Until Johnny cruelly laughed
He found an empty beer bottle
And then, broke it in half

He held the edges to my face
And I tried not to cry
He said, "Nobody tells Johnny
What to do with his time."

I knew he wouldn't hurt me
But what he meant was clear
Then Johnny whispered softly,
"Go away now, do you hear?"

His hard face twisted up a little
And a tear fell from his eye
He said, "Sis, you just don't know
What these wars are like."

Then, I fell on his neck and pleaded,
"Oh, Johnny, please don't go!"
He realized he'd shown a part of himself
He'd have rather left unknown

He was angry at himself and me
And he hissed words through his breath
"It's only cause we're blood-related
That's kept you from your death."

I felt so sad and scared for Johnny
That I turned and ran away
I ran into a church building
And I knelt down there to pray

I'd never said a prayer before
So I guessed at how to do it
I heard the sirens screaming
Before I was half-way through it

I ran out to meet the boys
Who had made it home all right
They were talking, mostly bragging,
About how they'd won the fight

Then, I said, "Where's Johnny?"
The talk completely died
The concrete was a magnet
For every pair of eyes

The oldest boy there,
Said to be a fearless killer,
Pushed a young boy forward
And said, "Go on, you tell her."

The young boy looked defiant
And he started to say, "No."
Then, he decided it was better
Just to do as he was told

He eyed the dirt and blood spots
That marked the clothes he wore
And he said, "Your brother Johnny,
He ain't coming home no more."

I Want to Feel Like a Man Again

This is much more than a crazy fad
Much more than finding a true love
Much more than reminiscing about position
And wild emails
We were supposed to escape
For no more than a few days
Bookkeeping for behind the lies
Of the junkyards of life
You had some money
You financed my whims
You watched me jump buildings
You gave me superhuman powers
When you disappeared
I was strangely lost
Wandering through rum and cake
To the sound of pool balls clacking
Did we create a monster?
Did we cross far too many lines?
I want to feel like a man again
Which is quite strange because I am
A woman

Lady Liberty, standing tall and free
Still and quiet, feet on solid ground
My eyes fill with tears
As I am overcome with awe
Of this amazing statute in my homeland
When the Murrah Building went down,
My sadness was multiplied
By the discovery that a fellow American
Had killed so many, so cold-heartedly
When the Twin Towers fell,
My sadness was multiplied
By the existence of hatred
My tears today are happy tears,
Patriotic tears,
Special tears
Of unity and appreciation
For freedom

Tornado Alley is Home

Tornado sirens sound in Norman, Oklahoma
I kick in to survival mode
Grab my cell, some water
Make it to the lowest level, a room without windows
Big day for television weather men
Advising of the tornado's path
Oh, no! The tornado is coming toward my house!
Electricity is lost and the TV dies
Scared, I text a friend
"Do you have a power?" I ask
I hear the rumble of the tornado passing by
Sparing me and my house this time
People in Moore, Oklahoma
Lose homes, lives, their children
I say a prayer for all the victims
And try to think of how to help
My friends from other States
Ask why I don't move
I love my town in Tornado Alley
All in life is a gamble
When April breezes flow
And sunshine begins to peek through clouds
Tornado season is coming, and I repeat a caution
Time to double-check the emergency supplies

Enough

I live in a house with windows,
But I can't see any children outside
They must be inside, watching television
I can't feel the wind on my face
But I can see the sky, and sometimes, that is enough
I work in an office with windows
I see traffic and gridlock outside,
people rushing, carrying briefcases
I can't feel the sun on my face
But I can see the sky, and sometimes, that is enough
I drive a car with windows
I see fellow drivers with cell phones
shoved next to their ears as they navigate carelessly
I can't see the moon
But I can see the sky, and sometimes, that is enough
I take a walk after work
I see children playing in the park
I feel the gentle breeze as the sun warms my face
Because it is dusk, I can also see an early moon
And I can see the sky, and always, that is enough

Pleasure and Pain

With whiskey on his breath
And a stagger in his walk
In his sloppy, beat-up shoes
With a slurring in his talk

Daddy took me in his arms
He swung me 'round through space
I laughed and kissed my Daddy
Until I spotted Mama's face

Her lips were pursed together
One brow was lifted high
Her eyes were full of fire
And the silent question, "Why?"

Then, Daddy turned to Mama
And shrugged his skinny shoulders
Mama turned to walk away
And she suddenly seemed older

I was still in Daddy's arms
But I struggled to be free
He recognized my effort
And set me down -- so carefully

I ran after Mama
She was gone long past the door
I turned back to Daddy
He was passed out on the floor

She didn't tell anyone
But she knew they did exist
Tiny fairies under flowers
Seen in the morning mist

She tiptoed through the moonlight,
Slept in a field of flowers
To be there when the fairies came
In the early morning hours

A rain of glitter awakens her
The fairies are revealed
They throw bold colors of laughter
Into the daisy field

The fairies make her promise
To tell no one where they dwell
She agrees delightfully
To embrace the fairy spell

Fruit of the Earth

Red sludge dripped from his mouth
His eyes were gritty with determination
The skin was pulpy
As he bit with relish
The tart sweetness was amazing
For this treat
Pulled from the earth
He was slimy with the juice
He had dared to follow passion
He looked at his hand
Holding a fresh tomato

Pie in the Sky

Cinderella had a fella
Snow White had a prince
Rapunzel had her tresses
It sort of all makes sense

All need to be rescued
By some handsome young man
Throughout fairy tales,
That is the standard plan

Independent Belle
Had her own life to lead
Her intelligence was proven
Because she liked to read

Of course, she then got captured
by the only Beast in town
But, at least to Belle's credit,
She didn't take it lying down

Eventually, Belle loves the Beast
As fairy tales always end
No matter how it's written
Love is the dividend

Life is a fairy-tale pursuit
For those who want an "ever after"
The improbability of such a chase
Fills the wise with laughter

The Hermit Life

Is my brain nature?
If so, why is it that
I only like the outdoors
From the indoors
I found a window
With a good view
Of jaybirds and robins
I look out
The window can open
with a twist pry bar
I never twist the bar
I look out, not in
Ever

A Dream of Schadenfreude

Is it wrong to want him to get a fine –
The driver who has lost his mind?
I drive the speed limit within the law
Behind me, he thinks this is a flaw
He whizzes past first chance he can,
Making a rude sign made with his hand
Then, he screeches at me, too
Just two words: a verb and "you!"
Is it wrong to hope that he gets stopped
By a law-abiding, street-wise cop?

No Sea for Plastic

I am overenthusiastic
And a tad dramatic
As I wax bombastic
About good ol' plastic

Plastic is found
In things all around
Cells, trucks and cars,
Medicines, mouth guards

Seat belts, car seats,
Air bags, sports cleats
Carpets, glitter,
Blankets, stickers

Let plastic use be tailored
Never be wayward
Plastic pollution is stoppable
When people are not responsible

Please be quite drastic
In recycling plastic
Keep it out of the trash
To prevent a future splash

Avoid any motion
Of plastic in the ocean
Recycling is key
Just avoid the sea

Officer Glands was armed with a warrant
Which was valid on its face
Mr. Anato was handcuffed and put into leg cuffs
His feet were shuffling back to the joint
Even the seasoned, brainy Glands
Got sick to his stomach
When the victim's bloody body was found
The scene was hair-raising

Mr. Anato had such nerve
To shoot a man in the heart
But he had no guts
He is a yellow-livered coward
Mr. Anato flapped his gums cheekily
Mouthing off about self-defense
But, despite the lip,
The evil heel was convicted of murder

The fingerprints, DNA, and a tooth,
Not to mention the eye-witnesses,
Nailed the case for the State
Oh, Mr. Anato. My!
Will you belly up, Mr. Anato,
To the death chamber?
Have your veins infused
Until your own heart stops?

Or will your gall be forgiven
By the secondary victims
And you'll go to a cell
For the rest of your life?

Walking on Pavement

I was proud of my ability to walk Broadway Avenue
To arrive at the play, second-row tickets
Proud because I had broken my foot and leg previously
A cast for months, then rehabilitated to learn to walk again
I asked the usher about the nearest restroom
The usher said, "Well, the bathrooms are upstairs,
But you can use the handicap restaurant on the first floor."
"Handicap?" I asked, surprised. I'd never thought of myself
In that way. Ever.
"Don't you have a walking problem?" The usher asked.
"How did you know?" I asked, my eyes wide with surprise.
"I saw you walking," the usher said.
We both laughed. Life is full of joy.

A macho bee with pollen power
Once met a pretty, lady flower
First, he nectar,
Then, he left her
Pregnant in less than an hour

All Play

Today
I will delay
Stay out of the fray
That is work

Tonight
I will delight
My appetite
With pizza

Tomorrow
Is coming soon
But my cocoon
Is cozy

I'm all play
Every day
Makes me
Exciting, but poor

I am Not a Hoarder

My house appears in disorder
Yet, I am not a hoarder
I just have a lot of clutter

I really will not tell a lie
You might call my abode a sty
So many things are piled so high

I am no hoarder, I must scream
Merely too stressed to deal with things
Oh, what tension this life brings!

Would a quick cure-all be to move?
But in the end, what would that prove?
I cannot get in the cleaning mood

Lack of neatness would clearly show
Pitching is not a skill I know
I would just pack the junk and go

I will stay planted in this mess
A house where more is never less
My bounty is complete excess

A search for things can make me gruff
Yet, I will hold on to all this stuff
Even when enough's enough

Me, a hoarder? I don't agree
I never know when I might need
This big, ol' gnarly tumbleweed

Launching a Campaign

I obtained more than a thousand signatures
That all agree
I should apprehend my soul
And re-design my life

Sally was a great dresser
Amy's clothes look affordable
Zed forgot to wear pants today

Rob won on *Jeopardy!*
Mary finished a sudoku rated easy
Bill lost all his money on scratch-offs

Tom works in genetics
Carol is a lab assistant
Kraken may be the missing link

Clase de Espanol

My teacher speaks so rapidly
While I Sit there so Vapidly
Learning Spanish is oh, so tough
Those gender verbs do make it rough
And what about the strangest plight
When double negatives are right?
There's two words to say "to be"
All these choices are haunting me
But, somehow, I am still compelled
To study, albeit overwhelmed
Although I sit here at a loss,
I refuse to say, "No Mas!"

Modern Science

I have always been aware of the true breakfast of champions
What is a better way to start the day
Than a large slab of gooey, chocolate cake
With a big glass of cold milk?
Now, some scientists have agreed with me.
I can't help but wonder
What took the professionals so long?

Conflicting Thoughts

If I were a wolf dressed like a sheep
Would I be able to sleep
Or would I be sorry about my deceit?

I told you while we were outside
I told you while we walked
I told you while we were inside
I told you while we talked

I told you with my voice
I told you with my eyes
I told you while we ate burgers
I told you while we ate fries

I told you in the car
I told you on the train
I told you on the bus
I told you on the plane

I told you on the phone
I told you face to face
I told you at the restaurant
I told you at my place

I told you at dinner
I told you at lunch
I told you on a whim
I told you on a hunch

I told you while we sat
I told you while we stood
I told you at the symphony
I told you in the 'hood

I told you while we danced
I told you while we dated
I told you while we laughed
I told you while we skated

I told you while you sighed
I told you on my turf
I told you while you coughed
I told you while we surfed

I told you during Games
I told you while we pedaled
I told you at the Olympics
I told you while we medaled
I told you while we sang
I told you while we recorded
I told you when our song was Number One
I told you while we snowboarded
I told you while I was President
I told you when you ran the country
I told you daily
I told you monthly

I told you at the baseball game
I told you during a line drive
I told you in the clouds
I told you during our sky dive

I told you on a boat
I told you on a raft
I told you at the zoo
I told you while we pet the giraffe

I told you during rain
I told you during sunshine
I told you during snow
I told you while we drank Moonshine

I told you like a harridan
I told you like a shrew
I told you, oh, so many times
I told you 90 times, times two

I told you while we knitted
I told you while we read
I told you while we thought
I told you while we bled

I told you during football
I told you during Jeopardy
I told you today
I told you yesterday

I told you with perfection diction
I told you very clearly
I told you ad nauseum
I guess you didn't hear me

I'm female color-blind like Ma
Dad's normal-visioned, so
My real Pop might not be Pa
Should I tell dear Daddio?

Shod in Sageness

Young Girl
Barefoot was perfect
Soft grass, tender Soles

Young Woman   82
Shoes were everything
Heels heightening, pain ignored

Wise Woman
Walking without Fear
Value known, comfort learned

Goodbye

I told him
That being in a relationship with him
Was like sitting in a car without an engine
I can sit there all day long
But the car is not going anywhere
He replied immediately,
 "You can always get out of the car."
Namaste, but I won't stay
This relationship is
Nevermore

Oh, to be in England!

College at Oxford gave me a new world-view
Testers walking down the street in caps and gowns
Draped with satin ribbons of various colors
Which symbolized the area of purported expertise
Beautiful gardens everywhere
The British love their flowers, yes?
Street vendors shouting to attract
Buyers of hot fish and chips
Or popcorn
Sweet or salty
Tea and scones served everywhere
For an afternoon treat
People actually saying, "Cheerio!"
I am now an Anglophile
But where is ice?
From fast-food to high-class food
No drinks are served with ice
Flying the long distance home
Provided a time when I could have
Savored my memories
Yet, all I could think about
Was that I could soon purchase a drink
Full of ice
Ice first, memories second

Moment in Time

There is a slight draft, a whispery breeze
Crossing by us
The wind provides
Friendly and playful
Competition against the heat of the sun on our faces
We stand at Strawberry Fields
In Central Park
With a group of strangers
Bonded by admiration for the concept
Of a songwriter's creativity
Even though the memorial
Has a dedicated quiet zone,
Some twenty-something males are strumming guitars
And actually singing the lyrics to "Imagine"
Words about not being the only dreamers
And the brotherhood of man
In that perfect instant,
In that unique convergence of time and space
And music and art and life
And wind and sunshine,
We are all at peace
The music is essential
And always will be

My best friends and I were leaving a restaurant
On something of a girls' night
But with teenage offspring plus their friends in tow
Once outside, we all noticed a gigantic round moon
So low in the sky we could almost touch it
Which prompted us women to sing, loudly and in unison,
"When the moon hits your eye
Like a big pizza pie"
Our children cowered in their embarrassment
Couldn't we see that there were other people outside?
Don't we know that Moms who sing in public are the worst?
Then, four young men on the bridge above us
Finished our lyric with outstretched arms
And in perfect harmony,
Signing, "That's amore!"
Instead of enjoying the beauty of that moment
Our children turned beet red, their ridiculous shame deepening
Which meant only that this was a perfect outing for us moms
Thanks, tenor, countertenor, baritone, and bass

The Way to a Man's Heart is Not Swedish Meatballs

I invited my new friend to my house to enjoy
Swedish meatballs
How hard could that be?
Noodles, sour cream, beef broth, and meatballs

Attempt 1:
I simmered the noodles in the sauce
Everything looked great, everything tasted awful
The noodles were beyond al dente
They were hard as rocks, inedible rocks
I should have cooked them first. Duh

Attempt 2:
He agreed to another try
I cooked the noodles first, then simmered them in the sauce
The smell was amazing, and I served them proudly
"Where are the meatballs?" He asked.
Oops! I had forgotten the meat.

Attempt 3:
I served him Swedish meatballs
By heating up a tv dinner
When I split this into two plates
Our portions were so small
And the taste was cardboard
"Thank you for trying," he said.
I noticed he only had one bite.

Attempt 4:
Forget Swedish meatballs
I ordered pizza for us
We were happy

My Personal Hero

Often, my brother likes to tease me
This is something that does not please me
Then, we climb a mountain one day,
And I see my brother in another way
When I stumble on a rock and begin to fall,
"I'll save you!" I hear my brother call
Somehow, he quickly rushes below me,
Catches me before I even skin a knee
Now, I can so clearly see
My brother is a super hero to me!

I Thought I'd Feel Older

Crossing the rubicon of age fifty
With all the strange past that I shed
My body's a bit like aged whiskey
But I'm still 27 in my head.

My leg cramps cause extreme pain
I'm slower getting out of bed
My ankles now predict rain
But I'm still 27 in my head

The crow's feet are longer and deeper
And my bottom has started to spread
I've become an irregular sleeper
But I'm still 27 in my head

On Monday, my stamina's askew
By Sunday, I hang on by a thread
Yet, I'm scrappy and always pull through
'Cause I'm still 27 in my head

Each trip to the doctor now ends
With a script for a new type of med
My pill count each day is at ten
But I'm still 27 in my head

Cataract surgery is scheduled
My arthritis is starting to smart
My mind is a bit more bedeviled
Oh, but I'm 27 in my heart

I refuse to let my age defeat me
I'll fight every day til I've bled
I'll always be all that I can be
And that's 27 in my head

The Sparrow

Once upon a primetime evening, while my TV screen was
    gleaming,
With many a new and crazy sitcom on my much-used screen —
While I watched, sometimes sleeping, suddenly there came a
    beeping,
Like a censor harshly beeping, beeping at the TV scene
"'Tis cable problems," I muttered, "beeping on my TV screen
Darkness is all I now have seen."

Ah, clearly, I recall I was watching the lineup of fall;
And now, much to my appall, my TV's screen had gone AWOL
I thought of calling Cable Town, but knew they'd only let me down
I chose to unplug the back, which always is the primary hack,
But vainly I had pulled the jack – I guess I somehow lost my knack
My TV screen still remained all black

To call myself one among authors when I waste time viewing TV
    offers
Mocked me, blocked me from writing words while I sat at my TV
    perch
When suddenly there came a sound of clashing, and the TV screen
    was flashing
The screen quickly went berserk, showing a Sparrow with a smirk
Who looked straight at me, and raspy voiced with a chirp,
Quoth the Sparrow, "Get to work!"

I was so surprised to see a TV Sparrow addressing me
"Birdie, forgive my pursuit of mirth, as I watch TV and gain some
    girth
The fact is I was relaxing, and your appearance is somewhat taxing
You showed up so strangely, appearing before this admitted dork,
The words to which you gave birth commanding me in a way that
    hurt."
Quoth the Sparrow, "Get to work!"

I was just a tad bit frightened, but then I also felt enlightened
I'll stop being such a lazy jerk, try to really find my worth
So I turned off my TV to dream of writing and no longer lurch
The silence was ever so sweet with TV taking a deserved backseat
Off with TV! On with computer! Time to now sign on to Word
As I told myself to, "Get to work!"

But Facebook was a rabbit hole. I once again had lost control
I couldn't leave the Twitter site. What could I do to make this
    right?
Could I call myself a writer when the future was not brighter?
Writing's too easy to eschew, but creativity I must renew,
And while I'm at it, I'll put down my fork
And force myself to get to work!

December Justice

'Twas the night before Christmas and all through the court
All the lawyers were stirring with last-minute work.
The judge was black-robed at the bench and declared,
"I hope that you lawyers are all well-prepared."

The prosecutor performed the voir dire with great care
In hopes that jurors would give the defendant "The Chair."
Other prisoners were nestled, all snug in their chains
With visions of freedom dancing through their brains.

But the one jolly defendant who was named Mr. Claus
Claimed innocence with such vigor that it gave them all pause.
Then, the prosecutor jumped up and stated real quick,
"This bum uses the alias St. Nick."

He was breaking and entering through the roof of a house.
He's guilty as sin! C'mon, fry the louse!
Oh, believe me, dear jurors, his bad deeds are real.
He even took in a bag for the things he would steal!"

As the prosecutor droned on in his "reversible" way,
The jurors were awakened by the sound of a sleigh.
Yes, out on the lawn there arose such a clatter
The spectators rushed out to see what was the matter.

Well, what would their wondering eyes behold
But a company of criminal defense lawyers unfold?
The sleigh was driven, of course, by Saint Justinian
who shouted, "That prosecutor cannot defeat any of us!"

Itching for action, the lawyers started to squirm
As Justinian commenced with a roll call of the firm.
He said, "We know Santa entered a not guilty plea.
Let's go show the D.A. how tough we can be."

Then Justinian told the judge, "Let's examine that sack."
And he dumped out the contents of Mr. Claus' pack.
Suddenly the floor was filled with great toys

That Mr. Claus was taking to all girls and boys.

"Why, this man wasn't stealing at all," said the judge.
"Instead, it's been proven, his heart's full of love."
The jurors applauded as Mr. Claus was released.
The prosecutor turned red and looked at his feet.
Claus said, "Oh, you've helped all right, Justinian.
But, how can I pay you? You know I am penniless."
Then, suddenly Claus brightened and slapped his big belly.
(And, of course, it shook like a bowl full of jelly.)

He reached into his bag while the lawyers waited agog
And pulled out a Best Buy catalogue.
"Order your pleasure, send the bill to the North Pole
In care of dear Santa . . . And now, I must go."

The defense lawyers were stunned because it seemed so bizarre
To be soon owning gifts they'd always admired from afar.
They were so pleased that they gave Santa their sleigh.
 (They all owned defense mobiles, anyway.)

And driving from sight, then shouted Santa Claus,
"Merry Christmas, Happy New Year, and Justice to All!"

TV is Raining

As children when we said,
"There's nothing on TV."
That was almost literally true
There were only three channels
One usually had sports
One usually had game shows
One usually had variety hours
Now, there is Amazon, Hula, Netflix, Youtube, Apple
New TV possibilities and opportunities are born each day
It is raining TV
A rain where we live umbrella-free
No one can sense the ions
No one can smell the newness
No one gets water-logged
Instead, embrace the time for today's poets

And the Winner Is . . .

The lights of the Vegas night
Shine ever so bright
Lights are seen from outer space
That just makes a case
Money to spend on so much neon
And why? For only one reason
The true logic, my friend,
Is that the house always wins

The lobbies of every Vegas hotel
Have some kind of story to tell
Manufactured wonder for you to see
Because they would like your money, please
The one-armed bandits play their part
To survive, you must be smart
What you must remember, my friend,
Is that the house always wins

Do not go down that dreaded path
Gambling is for those not good at math
Why throw all your hard-earned money away,
Causing your life to be full of dismay?
You can handle this all another way
By using your money for charity
Because all you need to know, my friend
Is that the house, for sure, will always win

Aromas

It's always a tease
With all that cheese
A cheese-arito
And a burrito
A bean taco
And a little guaco
I smell
Taco Bell!

Ode to a Tree

The Eastern Red Cedar
Strikes a pose like a leader
Making us need her
And wanting to feed her

Chronic Fatigue Syndrome
Has zapped all my strength
I leave the bed to eat a meal,
Then return to bed for more rest
So few people understand
So many people just think I am lazy,
Yet I am not even sure
I will have the strength
To finish writing this poe . . .

Thank you for reading!

-The End-